THIS PAPERBACK EDITION 1ST PUBLISHED IN 2014 BY DELERE PRESS LLP

ILLUSTRATIONS © SHARON YANG GE
TEXT © GABRIELLA TORRES
* * *
FIRST PUBLISHED IN 2014 BY DELERE PRESS LLP
BLOCK 370G ALEXANDRA ROAD #09-09 SINGAPORE 159960
WWW.DELEREPRESS.COM
DELERE PRESS LLP REG NO. T11LL1061K

ALL RIGHTS RESERVED

ISBN 978-981-09-2654-0

The Emergence of Brood III

Gabriella Torres

with paintings by PAYNK

DEDICATION

To Simon, Martha and Alfonso

ACKNOWLEDGMENTS

Thanks to Gina Myers, Dustin Hellberg and the Iowan Brood.

CONTENTS

Home Sweet Home

    by Gina Myers

Prelude

The Ascent

Transformation Stage

The Emergence of Brood III

(or The Iowan Blood)

Coda

HOME SWEET HOME

Gina Myers

When I think of the word "home," I can easily get lost in all that means to me, from considering and coping with the various traumas inflicted there—both real and imagined—to reflecting on youth and remembering the desire to grow, to grow up and to leave. Those stagnant summer days where everything was slowed down and my friends and I were left just waiting for our lives to begin. Of course, by life we meant on our terms: the life that begins when you become an adult (or near-adult) and seize control, head out on your own, and take the world on. This version of life always included leaving home, and often it meant getting as far away from there as possible.

And yet, the joke was—at least for me—that once I left I would continue to be haunted by home. And this haunting can trick you into thinking you want to return. It can make you think of only the good times and it makes home appear as a refuge from whatever present you currently find yourself in. But as Gertrude Stein reminds us, "There is no there there." We can't go back. And if we do, we will find it changed, sometimes beyond recognition. The feeling we're yearning for is always and forever out of reach.

*

Sometimes people feel like home—there's an immediate connection, a comfort, a sense of deep understanding as if you've always known this other person. Gabriella Torres and I met in graduate school and became fast friends. Her Iowa felt like my Michigan; her struggles mirrored my own. It was as if I'd always known her, and I never had to explain myself to her to be understood. She understood the things that haunted me and continued to shape the person I was. She became my sister. A sense of home.

*

The poetry in *The Emergence of Brood III* is a haunted poetry. The poems create a space where the ghosts of the past and the ghosts of what could have been co-mingle. The ghost of Iowa, of Torres' childhood, looms large. While the story of the seventeen year cicadas have captured the attention of many, I have no doubt that it is because Brood III is known as the Iowan Brood that Torres was drawn to this subject—that the idea, like the cicadas falling from the twigs, dug itself down into her brain and wouldn't relent until it saw light. The cicadas serve as a means for Torres to transport herself back home to Clinton, IA.

*

Though the project spans the lifecycle of the cicadas, the heart of it is after the emergence, when after seventeen years the cicadas break through and begin life, when "The sky breaks. / To reveal another sky." Of course, to be a teenager is to live a life of extremes. Everything feels like a matter of life or death. Torres writes, "You are 17, a teenaged dream. / After all. / It's time to get your kicks. / Or die trying." In the world of the poem, faith is a matter of survival, or survival a matter of faith. Everything is intensified as the speaker goes from "ghost to wolf," as scars are left on branches, and wounds left on wings. After seventeen years of lying in wait, the cicadas experience life fast and furious: "To be at once beginning and end."

*

The life of the teenager, even with its extremes, is ghostlike. You're not fully present, always longing for something else, waiting on what comes next: "You were gone before you even began."

*

It's only distance that allows us to look back. *The Emergence* is Torres' song "[t]o the cul-de-sac, the empty swing set, the tree house overrun with rot." She sees "kids on bicycles peddl[ing] back to the sounds of dinertime bells and the loss of something they can't quite grasp." It's this loss of innocence—the loss of something unidentifiable that some people hope to rediscover when they return home. But Torres' writing is smarter than that and knows the thing that cannot be grasped never will be.

*

Torres reminds us, "Summer [is] just a fraction of a life but carries everything in it." I'm reminded of the fable where the cicada sings all summer and doesn't prepare for winter. Torres claims, "The summer only endless for as long as you can sing." Recently I found a single cicada wing on the floor at work. I took a photo of it and posted it to *Instagram*. Someone told me it was good luck. Elsewhere I've read that the cicada is a symbol of insouciance. For Torres it seems to be something else entirely—something full of potential, something intensely (if only briefly) teeming with life, something darkly beautiful that exists in the liminal. Perhaps it's a good luck totem after all.

PRELUDE

Life begins with a fall.

Specifically from a branch or a twig.

Then we hit the ground, digging. We dig and dig until the darkness shuts out any memory of the light.

Who remembers milliseconds anyway?

In the dirt our wings are contained, less glass and more arbitrary.

                                          Unspecified value.

In the dirt, we dig and dig until we hit a root.

That's when life really begins.

We attach ourselves to the root and drink up the juice.

> One part timeline,
> three parts inheritance
> (worm decay,
> bird bones, regrets).

We drink the root juice and filter through history –root vampires – drinking root blood.

We live like this for 17 years.

Suspended.

> Until we look for the light.

THE ASCENT

It's easier than it sounds.

Really.

You just look up and climb.

        Out of the darkness and into life.

You are 17, a teenaged dream.

After all.

        It's time to get your kicks.

Or die trying.

Is there a word for digging up?

Nothing can prepare you for the light.

                                        Not for all the root juice—

There's an almost spiritual quality.

It's an act of faith. Or survival.

                                        Is there a difference?

Just climb. This is what you didn't know you were waiting for.

This is what you didn't know

There's movement in the dirt.

I can hear it all around me, restless.

Maybe the bird bones are coming back to sing.

>The bitterness
>of broken beaks.
>And other hits.

The ground is heating up and I feel this ache.

Where all the joints meet.

Pushing me away from the roots.

Towards an incredible lightness.

>Or some great fantastic.

You tell me.

In other words.

There will be no more digging.

                                        So long root juice.
                                        So long dirt parade.

I'm moving on up. For a piece of the light.

It's simple, really. The sky breaks.

To reveal another sky.
                                        Excuse me while—

My eyes adjust to a million burning sparklers.

I don't care if it's endless.

Just so long as it's mine.

TRANSFORMATION STAGE

The skin breaks along the seam of the back.
For a moment there is nothing but stillness.

                              This split from
                              darkness to light.
                              From earthbound
                                      to levity.

It's like that.

                              Life as a nymph.

Some barely recognizable song.

A melody you remember remembering.

                              At some point.

The soundtrack to your life until.

This new kind of atmosphere.

From pulse to sonar. From darkness to blue.

Let's hang here, suspended, and consider the possibilities.

                                            Into the great wild.

Open until the skin hardens.

                                                  At ease.

Emerge your delicate voice.

A turn. Head straight up for the leaves.

THE EMERGENCE OF THE BROOD III
(OR THE IOWAN BROOD)

We sit in the silence of the heat like kids at summer camp sweating out their adolescence, still and close.

This is how you become an adult.

Six days in waiting, from ghost to wolf.

Hungry like—

The anticipation of the very first sound. It starts softly, then grows. The hum of the song, the echoes of the heat expanding like wings. Your delicate membranes catching every last beat.

You know where you are.

Unmeasured timeline like alien or God.

                                    Drone like the universe.
                                    Buzz like outer space.

This is your song. The only one you'll ever sing.

Summer just a fraction of a life but carries everything in it.

    So much hinging on the chorus in the trees.
                    I know there are others calling.

Come together. Follow me.

Our voices intertwine until
we've woven a net that stretches across the
immediate sky.

Somewhere between the heat and the stars
there is us.

                        Where you feel it most
                            is where you feel it.

In this hollow abdomen there are infinite
gestures.

I'm trying to meet you. I want to hear you
sing in equal tempered semitones.

                        Each half step another
                           intimation. A subtle
                            tying of knots or a slit
                                 in the wrist.

The summer only endless for as long as you
can sing.

Forget the words you thought you knew.

All wrapped up in chorus. There is nothing
more to believe than this.

No one prepares you for the sound of your own voice.

To hear the decibels resound, expand and consume all other traumas.

                                                Get back.

Against a deafening wall. There is no recourse.

Nature has the upper hand, so we live by the nights that burn themselves into the leaves, scars on the branches, wounds on the wings.

                                    The heat a drug
                                      to sing and fly to.

The life of a prime number.

                                              Add it up.

This is what you get.

Only the lonely will fall from the trees with nothing to give but five little eyes.

Once you get hit you never go back.

    A stomach turned to stone. Your petrified youth.

Everything you lived for rendered void. There's no time for questioning yourself. The champions of loss but never regret.

Your contribution.

                                Such a pretty song.

Reach out in the darkness.

Fade out.

You click your wings and I respond with a vibration that brings us closer to the brink.

                                   We will live forever.

Our reverb one infinite echo as giant as our hearts.

At least for now.

                                   Or until the chorus kicks in.

This new song more intimate with a shake of your head.

                 You'll only ever be as old as this night and as lovely as the sound of your heat.

You are the sum of the first four primes.

Though odd, you are the least random.

A life cycle of limited song. The number of syllables in a summer haiku.

If you think about it, what makes us arbitrary makes us beautiful.

        I am being simple.

I eat my vowels and whisper consonants across continents.

I boomerang my heart so that it will come back to me.

        I am saying nothing.
        I reserve my rights.

The heat becomes oppressive this time of year. It holds you down by your antennae wrists and breathes its hot air all over your face. You would choke if you could choke. If you had air in the lungs.

        It presses its weight on top of you
           until you pass out.

All other sounds consumed by the oncoming wave.

We act like it was some sort of fever dream the next day.

                                        But we are as lost as ever.

Now it is clear we are boundless.

                                        Unrestrained and inevitable.

Those were the exact words.

Eye contact impossible during the day.

                                          Who could stand it?

We recover on the bark of trees, nostalgic for our underground nursery rhymes. Hey diddle-diddle.

If I knew now what I knew then.

                              But that is impossible.

The bats begin their vespertine run, which means we all know what's coming while kids on bicycles peddle back to the sounds of dinnertime bells and the loss of something they can't quite grasp.

                              Peddle faster.
                              Chase it down.

Let me speak in monosyllables:

When it ends, there will just be you.

One milky blue eye, one fire red.

                        One in a million emergences.

It's been known to happen. Call it inheritance.

                        The luck of the draw.

A song caught in the back of your throat. It chokes you from the inside, pulling your tongue back inside of you until you swallow yourself whole.

To be one life amongst multitudes.

Wishing you had never looked up.

These are the songs we sing.

The buzz that fluctuates and sticks to the skin like sweat or heat from the breath.

> We live by night
> to outlive the living.
> We live to fuel
> one thousand parades.

The odd thing is that no one stops to wonder if there are others down below tucked in amongst the roots and bone decay, matter-making matter, that will one day emerge.

> As if you could break a cycle
> like so many blades of grass
> or delicate wrists.

There's no point speaking in hypotheticals.

We are born without teeth and no way of knowing.

It has always ever been a matter of time.

Is there anything else?

Time to make sounds, to make waves, to make your way to another field.

      You were gone before you even began.

Pulsing throughout your feeble wings, your hollowed out heart. Resonating through the heat. Everybody caught it. Everybody joined in.

                        The singing aggregation
                          a kick in the head.

What followed were a sequence of bacchanal nights better left in the branches of the young maple tree planted by somebody's father.

A series of little suicides littering the lawn.

        To be hunted down by a dog or a cat.

We build up our narrative from what remains.

Make wounds in the flesh of adolescent twigs.

CODA

Sing us a song. So we did.

To the cul-de-sac, the empty swing set, the tree house overrun with rot.

                                      Like our abdomens,
                                      hollowed and spent.

One suburban summer, we swallowed it whole. The branches bending underneath the weight, the culmination of a million little desires burning holes into the leaves.

                        To be at once beginning and end.

Until we dry up and, quietly, fall.

Gabriella Torres is the author of the chapbook *Sister* (Lame House Press, 2005). Her poems have appeared in *Cannibal, Past Simple, Sink Review, MiPOesias, Bateau Press, Dorado, H_NGM_N,* and *Cocunut Magazine.* Originally from Iowa, she spent several years in New York City before making her way to Seoul, South Korea, where she currently resides.

PAYNK is an illustrator from Singapore. She is a regular contributor to Kult Magazine and at Organization of Illustrators Council events. Her works have also been featured in Nylon Magazine, the Substation, Blackberry Poster Society and more. It is also important to note that she is addicted to peanut butter.

www.ingramcontent.com/pod-product-compliance
Lightning Source LLC
Chambersburg PA
CBHW041957150426
43193CB00003B/47